More praise for Chase Dimock:

"Chase Dimock's Sentinel Species is bursting with life. The animals, insects, and plants that populate these poems--alive or dead, thriving or in decline--provide startling gateways into explorations of human existence. Dimock's poems examine memory, culture, and the fundamental yearning that comes with being alive through a joyously dizzy array of extended metaphors and associations. These are poems that speak to the fundamental dignity of the living, and celebrate the emotional and intellectual flora and fauna of the everyday."

-James Brubaker, author of *The Taxidermist's Catalog* and *Black Magic Death Sphere: (science) fictions.*

More praise for Chase Dimock:

"Honest, clear sighted, and masterfully written, this is a beautiful and important book which gives voice to the creatures that we love and may lose. Chase's remarkable knowledge of endangered species is coupled with a charm, wit and inventiveness which makes this a delightful read and one which engenders empathy by showing what we share with the animal world, not least in the shape of Koko the Gorilla who asks god *why she was given knuckles that drag the ground and a mind that questions the sky.*

                -Anna Saunders, CEO Cheltenham Poetry Festval
                     and author of six collections
                     including *Ghosting for Beginners*
                     (*Indigo Dreams*).

Sentinel Species

A Bestiary of Poems by Chase Dimock

Stubborn Mule Press
Devil's Elbow, MO
stubbornmulepress.com

Copyright © Chase Dimock, 2020
First Edition 1 3 5 7 9 10 8 6 4 2
ISBN: 978-1-952411-30-4
LCCN: 2020944555

Cover image: Dallas Robinson
Author photo: Chase Dimock
All rights reserved. No part of this publication may be reproduced or transmitted in any form or by any means, electronic or mechanical, including photocopying, recording or by info retrieval system, without prior written permission from the author.

Poems in this book have previously been published in: *Apeiron Review, The Cape Rock, Funicular Magazine, Flyway, The Gateway Review, The Museum of Americana, New Mexico Review, The Northridge Review, San Pedro River Review, Santa Ana River Review, Saw Palm, Trailer Park Quarterly, Bombay Gin* and *Waccamaw.*

I want to thank the following people for their generosity and brilliance in helping me put this book together:

To Mike James and Daniel Crocker for their feedback on many of the poems in this book and for their consistent support and encouragement while I developed as a poet.

To Mary Angelino for providing insightful feedback on the manuscript and helping me to sculpt it into its final form.

To Dallas Robinson for his stunning visual interpretation of my poetry. I hope everyone judges my book based on its cover.

And to the late Okla Elliott, whose legacy I have tried to keep alive on *As It Ought To Be Magazine*. I'm not sure I would have ever found the courage to write and publish without his encouragement years ago.

Table of Contents

Part I: The One With The Waggly Tail

His Master's Voice / 1

Coming Out to a Spider / 2

Nativity Flood / 3

Imitation Unicorns / 5

Sea Swarming / 7

Flutterbys / 9

Gladdis: A True Televised Story / 11

Ray Cats / 15

The Coroner as a Child / 17

The Mink Cries White Diamonds / 19

Burying my Dog Behind the Ronald Reagan
   Presidential Library / 21

Patient Zero / 24

The Blobfish / 27

The Rat King / 30

A Flamboyance / 32

The Afterlife of Origami / 33

A Standard Monkey Funeral on Sunset Boulevard / 34

Oxygen is Flowing to the Mask / 36

My Dog Begs for Something that Will Kill Her / 38

Part II: Vegetative States

Medicinal Plants / 43

Cactus Needle / 45

A Banyan Tree / 46

Drought in Los Angeles / 48

American Gothic / 49

Haying / 50

Spilt Milk / 51

A Boy and His Piñata / 53

Hollywood Camouflage / 55

Victory Garden / 57

Produce in a Pandemic / 59

Part III: Zoonomia

Your Mother Doesn't Want You Wasting
   Color Film on Zebras / 65

The Inquisitor's Parrots / 67

Great Hall of the Bulls / 68

The Vulture and the Little Girl / 70

The Law of the Tongue / 72

The Desert Snail at Once Awoke
   and Found Himself Famous / 74

P.T Barnum Presents the Egress / 76

The Art of Preparing, Mounting,
   and Stuffing the Skins / 78

A Taxidermist and a Mortician Walk into a Bar / 80

Bees that Feed on Human Tears / 81

Coal Mine Canaries / 82

Earthquake Weather / 84

Shooting the Janitor / 85

The Falling Iguanas / 87

The Battle of the Zoo / 89

Koko the Gorilla Signs in the Afterlife / 91

The One With The Waggly Tail

His Master's Voice

Diagnosed with Old Dog Vestibular Syndrome,
Bailey walks with his head cocked sideways
in a permanent question I cannot answer.
Only at a skew does his world become level,
always one misstep from falling off the planet.

I stumbled from my room, hung over. His
obedient eyes swirled to match my wobbling
steps. The carpet fell from beneath us, the walls
folded over, and we landed on the ceiling.

As he stood over my body, I saw Nipper
on the old RCA logo, staring perplexedly
into the metal horn of an old record player
as his dead master's voice rang through.

Was RCA selling the promise of an afterlife
grooved in vinyl? At 78 revolutions, a portal
opens and we swirl back into existence for
dogs who don't believe the instinct of grief.

But I know Bailey would follow the record's
rotation, circling his head around and around
until dizzy, and fall to find me under the table.
We hold on together, and watch our ancestors
in the constellations spin us around the sun.

Coming Out to a Spider

Because she spun a downy web
in the corner of my bedroom
and sat patiently unperturbed.

Because it counted as saying it aloud to
a living being, a body of matter and feeling,
even if the words were for myself, sticky
strings pulled from my lips in which
I'll always have to make my home.

Because I could practice stuttering beneath
the stare of eight eyes at once.

Because she was not Charlotte, and I
would not wake up to *Some Homo*
or *Fruity* written in her web.

Because she had seen all the evidence:
my sister's boy band issues of Teen People
smuggled into my bedroom, the night tremors
mumblings of Dylan, Trevor, Kevin
in the desiring vocabulary of sleep.

Because I am still afraid of spiders
and could pretend it was her that I feared.

Because I could smash the witness
with a newspaper, smear the blame across
the wall, and wash myself in the cleansing blood
of the clorox bottle.

Nativity Flood

When the basement flooded, boxes
of Christmas decorations disintegrated
and the ornaments floated to the surface.
A yule tide ocean of shipwrecked
Hallmark keepsakes, plastic reindeer
swimming through the flotsam of tinsel
and ropes of fake garland, Rudolph
refusing to go down with the sleigh.
Baby Jesus in his manger bed like a lifeboat,
a refugee searching for the shore.
The nativity sheep sank like the dinosaurs
we learned showed up too late for the ark.

After we pumped the basement dry, we shoveled
wads of soggy wrapping paper, tossed
unraveled, limp bows. The ink ran off
years of christmas cards. We kept a list:

> 1. of people to whom we sent cards
> 2. people we got cards from
> 3. and people who did not reciprocate.
> They had three years to send a card
> before they were removed from the list.

Their sins washed away as wet piles of greetings
filled trash bags along with tense knots of christmas
lights we could never untangle, a plaster dove ornament
I painted poorly so I could go back to playing video games,
Joseph's cotton ball beard, through which I spoke his few
inconsequential lines in the Christmas pageant.

We kept just the stockings, hung them to dry
on the mantle, and gazed at the fire next time.
We set to repopulate the earth with gingerbread men
burnt legs and misshapen heads now a point of pride,
while the ceramic magi and camel we never found
kept searching the basement ceiling for the star.

Imitation Unicorns
- *For Nellie*

When I first held you
I watched Unicorns prance
in soft fleecy pink across
your onesie as your dreaming
breathing belly rose in and out
lifting them off into the infinite
pastel possibilities of infancy.

I wondered when you'll start
sorting your fairy tale menagerie
into fact and fiction, when Z
will still be for Zebra, but U
will have to settle for Urchin
or the Unspotted Saw-whet Owl
the Unlined Giant Chafer Beetle
the Unstreaked Tit-Tyrant
or any number of animals
defined by what they lack.

Will you still marvel at
the Unadorned Rock Wallaby
despite his lack of adornment?

Will you still respect
the Unarmored Threespine Stickleback
despite her vulnerability?

Will you accept substitutes?

The fencing Narwhal
swashbuckling the Baltic
more weaponized than majestic

The Hornbill who flies like pegasus
but shrieks, fighting for figs in the trees

When Marco Polo first laid eyes
on a Rhinoceros in the land of Basma
he wrote, Unicorns are
> *altogether different from what we fancied.*

He bemoaned, Unicorns are
> *not in the least like that which our stories tell of.*
> *They delight much to abide in mire and mud.*
> *Tis a passing ugly beast to look upon.*

I hope you never use myth as your measure.

When you gaze at the Unicorn trotting through
the frosted cupcake mountains on your Lisa Frank
Trapper Keeper, know that fantasy is a projection
of our inner colors, on a world both grey, and yet
so brilliant, we can't see all the light in the spectrum.

And most of all, humor your uncle
when he pulls a mule to your birthday party,
straps a rainbow painted corn cob to its head.
When you ride old Wilbur into a sunset that stops
at the fence in your backyard, know he did the best
Unicorn impersonation his old bones could carry.

Sea Swarming

Pismo clams strewn across the beach
a swarm of butterflies, petrified midair
and fallen to the sand. The surf laps
at orange and purple striped wings
twitching in the waves, too sodden
with saltwater to return to flight.

Sweating raw chicken pink, hurrying
I hunch over, collect greedy handfuls,
pennies from a fountain, stolen wishes
jingling in my pocket, until I realize
I am alone. Not even miserly gulls
feign interest in my scavenging.

My grandfather first brought me to the beach
at night. I could see only Mars on the horizon:
a red safety light atop the oil derricks pumping
crude from beneath the depths. He promised
the dark snarling of the black waves would stock
the coast with shells from Hawaii and Japan.

I demanded we wake at dawn. In my sleeping bag
I squirmed like a caterpillar fighting the chrysalis
of slumber, cringing to the rumble of the ocean's fist
tossing and shattering my shells, imagining swarms
of children at sunrise pulling hair, pushing
and shoving in ways I could not compete.

At morning, a humid sun steamed through
the overcast canopy; shells glimmered untouched.
I ran with my ice cream bucket for a pail, expecting
the schoolyard to spill over the dunes at any moment
but they remained barren, save for sandpipers sifting
the flotsam for the sandcrabs I stepped upon.

You cannot hear the ocean when you hold
a bivalve to your ear. They splay themselves, two
pearled palms cupped in a handcuffed offering. No
spiraling channels inside for the breeze to become
trapped and howl. Just an open locket with a photo
so sea weathered, you cannot recognize your face.

Flutterbys

My Grandfather told me
a butterfly my net misses
is called a flutterby.

Furnished with twigs, milkweed, and moss
my pickle jar habitat lacked nothing,
except a butterfly and air holes.

I flailed in the air, empty net straining the sky
within arm's reach, as the Monarch flew past
the visual barrier of a blue horizon, the reflection
of my eyeball on the opposite side of the empty jar.

I've learned never to look directly into absence.
A dead aquarium frames your profile like
you're on TV, a nature show broadcasting
all the belly up goldfish you struggle to scoop.
The stainless steel bottom of an empty water bowl
reflects the face no longer licked.

I earned an F on the habitat project, hid my
pickle jar in the desk rather than submit it.
When you exhibit a jar filled with inquiry
but no specimen, you become the subject,
the amoeba pressed flat beneath the glass.
They watch you struggle to divide, and point
as your clone swims away from you.
The guinea pig in the wheel who thought
all his cycling would get him back to Peru.

Better to deny the beauty you thought
you could hold, deny you ever envisioned
the monarch, foot caught in the ravines
of your fingerprints, wings fanning rainbow
pixels glittering your hands. Far better
to hold the magnifying glass above the ants,
balance the salt shaker above the snail,
than to be seen holding treats
for a dog more interested in his own behind.

Gladdis: A True Televised Story

I.
Ears perked up, tongue panting,
Gladdis sat in the cab of a truck
parked on the freeway overpass
as her owner, Daniel Victor Jones
unfurled a tarp big enough
for the news helicopters to see scrawled
in crudely spattered spray paint:

>*HMO's are in it for the money!!*
>*Live free,*
>*love safe*
>*or die.*

Reading from a TV screen
tucked miles away in a suburb,
my siblings and I did not know
what an HMO was, but we could tell
they were the bad guys. Bad like
Elmer Fudd and Yosemite Sam
and all cartoon villains
preempted that afternoon
to show this breaking news.

II.
You want to believe,
Gladdis knew this was going to be the end
as she remained dignified for the news cameras
in a stoicism her owner could not possess.
When we are allowed to write the words
of our own epitaphs, we maintain the illusion
that death is our volition.

She had seen Daniel erode into despair.
His HIV diagnosis was still thought of
as a death sentence by his friends.
He felt abandoned by a health care system
that promised drugs, but no treatment for stigma.
When a growth began to protrude from his neck
impotence and shame devoured his reason
faster than any cancer.

She co-starred in his suicide video,
curled up beside him on his threadbare couch
as he said to the camcorder's sterile lens:

> *I'm not going to fight the disease.*
> *It has affected my neurological system.*
> *I'm not going to end up crazy*
> *I'm a dead man.*
> *See ya.*

III.
Was Gladdis reassured
when Daniel returned to truck,
took a sip of his beer,
and scratched her behind the ear?

With one hand still on the scruff of her neck,
he detonated a Molotov cocktail and a silent
eruption of flames rushed from the cab,
her faint figure obscured by the fire.
You could sense Gladdis's resigned betrayal
when Daniel bolted from the truck, clothes ablaze
and frantic, unable to bear the immolation.
He left her to die alone, too engulfed
in his own agony to return
her final look of abandonment.

Dazed stumbling partially naked
before the pot boiling narration
of the news anchor like the play by play
announcer at a football game,
Daniel looked up to the sky,
a supplication, hoping the cameras
knew to zoom in tight as he propped
the shotgun under his neck.

I heard,
but only in my pubescent imagination,
the sound effect of the blast,
his head whipped to the asphalt,
his consciousness evaporating.

The news anchor finally broke the
indifferent ticking of the helicopter blades:

> *You do not know*
> *how much*
> *we regret*
> *that*
> *that*
> *got on the air.*

The TV spared us the cleanup,
the bagging of the body
and the shoveling of the remains
as it returned to the cartoons.
An anvil fell on Daffy Duck's head
and I felt his beak, wings, and bones
shatter for the first time.

Ray Cats

The half life of our waste is longer
than the span of our language.
In 10,000 years, long after the American flag
has fallen and the breath of the last English speaker
has evaporated into the air, our nuclear byproducts
will be more than 50% potent, still toxic beneath
the sands of Nevada, where suburban civilization
will sprawl, then ebb.

How will we warn the heirs to our radiation
in a language yet to be uttered? To answer,
scientists and linguists created Nuclear Semiotics:
a study into the universal signification
of danger and fear.
Bastide and Fabbri proposed breeding Ray Cats:
a species that glows ominously when exposed
to radiation. Fabulists and artists would be tasked
to create a mythology of the illuminated cat
as nuclear harbinger, knowing stories and sculpture
survive well past the life of the culture in which
they were first imagined.

When I see Charley staring blankly at a wall
I wonder if he's transfixed by an isotopic decay
only he can see. Those glowing yellow eyes
trying to tell me about something invisibly
denaturing my DNA. When he dashes through
the house at 3 AM, can he hear some kind of
high pitched geiger counter racing, telling me to

run? When he begs me to rub his belly, only
to claw and bite my hand, is it the nitrates
in my hot dog? The aluminum in my deodorant?
The particulates of smog seeping into the room?
I try to translate the cuneiform Charley scratches
down my arms. The marks puff red in a warning
I cannot read.

The Coroner as a Child

From the child's seat in the grocery cart
he reached to poke the plastic-wrapped beef.
A cold spun yarn of muscle,
pooled blood around his finger.
His grandmother's reprimand disturbed
the careful application and release of pressure
and as she yanked his arm away
he squirmed, slipped, and punched
his finger through the cellophane:
a bullet hole in an unfurled animal.

She made him pay for the meat
with a five dollar bill still kept
in his birthday card.
On the car ride home
he held the wounded beef in his lap,
feeling the warming blood spilling
into the bag and sloshing over his legs
in rhythm with the potholes.

He watched Grandma fry the meat
into patties, grease spattering
pinprick burns across their arms.
Her lecture on wasting food and
children starving in Ethiopia
muffled by the sizzle.
The smoke visible in the kitchen light
blanketed the antiseptic lemon smell
on his twice-washed hands as
the beef's skinned knee color
seared into a cadaverous grey.

> *Do you think they are safe to eat now?*
>
she asked, answer already in mind.
He nodded without reason.
> *A-HA!*
>
She cut a patty in half.
> *Still Pink!*

At the dinner table his burger was served
dissected into three blackened parts,
leaving charcoal trails on the bun.
Even a ketchup transfusion could not
reanimate the cremated remains
as they sanded his teeth.
She counted his bites, 1, 2, 3 to 50
before motioning to swallow
the puree of meat, bread, condiment,
and textured filler.

When she cleared the dishes,
he snuck outside to the garbage can,
and dug out the grocery bag
peppered with old coffee grounds,
and sticky with brown oxidized blood.
He stuck his finger in the gristle smeared
on the styrofoam tray. The taste was metallic
like a razor blade inside a Candied Apple
handed by a stranger on Halloween,
and just as sweet.

The Mink Cries White Diamonds

Not the ropes of jeweled necklaces
cascading down the mink stole
though they glisten like tears
beneath the chandelier light, and run
sparkling tracks down the gown
from where its head once sat.

But the perfume by Elizabeth Taylor
Every Valentine's Day in the commercial
      These have always brought me luck
The mist of opulence at Nordstrom's entrance
that delouses the public as we bring the stench
of Hot Dog on a Stick in our t-shirts and jeans.

Yesterday, I read that the wild mink
is aggressively territorial, never cohabitating
with the same sex, only letting a female in
to mate. They plot their boundaries
with their excrement and patrol the borders
of their marsh for the waft of an intruder.

You told me your mother's cedar chest
was meant not only to repel moths
when she locked the stole deep inside.
Had she seen you shooting your pop gun
then wearing the mink on your head
king of the wild frontier, driving out Indians
and remembering the Alamo, the stole
would still be draped on a velvet hanger.

But she caught you swaying and pouting your lips
in the mirror as it draped around your neck,
luxuriating in the generations of fragrance,
the come hither perfume that lured
a great-grandfather, the pheromones
of thin cigarette smoke and sweet vermouth
the pettable softness conjured into view.

The stole has been hibernating for decades
in the bottom of the chest, absorbing the musty
remnants of memory: heirlooms that tarnish
when we no longer want to see ourselves
reflected in their history. Though you have a key,
you know the mink can awaken at any moment
and slash you with his manicured claws.

Burying my Dog Behind the Ronald Reagan Presidential Library

In the hills of my hometown,
I have witnessed the burials
of two house cats
a golden retriever
and the 40th President
of the United States of America.

Beau stayed alive long enough
for me to arrive home from college.
Glaucoma fogged his vision
horseflies lapped at his sores,
his tail too limp to swat them away.

The rock I placed above his grave
is missing, probably blown down
the dusty cliff by the Santa Ana winds.
I replaced it with a half drunk PBR
the last time I hiked up the hill.
Across the ravine, Reagan's library
is visible from a golf course
and a trailer park.

When Reagan died, an old man
spent two weeks on the freeway overpass
holding up an autographed picture
burning jelly bean shaped carcinoma
into his bald head with not so much
as a puffy VFW Post hat to shield the sun.

He remembers the colonial eighties,
the white flight from LA that formed Simi Valley
that built a community of upper middle class
upper middle managers.

Makeshift memorials in Reagan's honor
marked the significant street corners.
Red White and Blue dyed 7-11 carnations
and jet ink home printed Reagan photos
replaced the weathered remnants
on telephone poles. Tattered posters of lost pets,
campaign posters, frayed yellow support our troops
ribbons and the wax of a candlelight vigil
where Joey was hit on his bike.

The memorials popped up everywhere
that seemed vaguely patriotic:
in front of the post office, city hall,
the police station and beneath the 50 feet
of rippling stars and stripes waving
in the parking lot of the Chevrolet dealership.

There was a collective sense of loss
though not everyone was quite sure
what they were missing.

I could see my house
from the helicopter footage,
the parade of Limousines
and hearses filled with dignitaries
as Secret Service agents
guarded a corpse with their lives.

Larry King stared silently
at me from the TV waiting
for some kind of grieving .
I didn't know how to muster
as I stroked a cat in my lap
who did not know it too,
in four months, would join
the president and Beau
in the hills.

Patient Zero

Ask any educated lycanthropist
and they will tell you
the one and only way to kill a werewolf
is a single silver bullet.

And so in turn
we expect all monstrosities,
mythic or real
all multiplying mutations,
benign or infectious
to originate from a single, traceable point
and arch toward a predictable end.

In High School,
the football coach taught all the health classes
and though he used no anatomy charts, we learned
everything from made for TV movies.
Meredith Baxter made the tragedy of Bulimia knowable
in a way the science of a textbook never could.
But when it came to Sex Ed, coach broke into lecture:

AIDS was caused by a bisexual doing it with a monkey

As an adult, I have heard
the well-rehearsed monkey mythology,
and though there are many ways man
could have come into contact
with a monkey's bodily fluids,
we always return to sex
as if the disease had to be a punishment.

Knowing no meaning to our suffering offers us no redemption.
We fear the indifference of a virus as much as its symptoms.

All mythologies need a villain.
If the frustrated labor of scraping out a living on a hostile earth
can be traced to a single woman picking forbidden fruit,
then all the anxieties, shame, and tormented desires of the flesh
can be blamed on the deviant rustling in the bushes.

The villain had to be bisexual.
Not homo or hetero.
Not the devil you know
or the devil you suspect,
but a shapeshifter.

At 14, with my bleached hair
and boy band pleather plants,
I felt implicated by this history,
called to atone for these sins
scrawled on the chalkboard.
I was to blame for the fall of Rome,
the erosion of America's family values,
and the astonishing 761 show run
of *Starlight Express* on Broadway.

In college, I learned of the conspiracy theories:
AIDS was concocted in a government lab
to eradicate the gay rights movement.
Complete with apocryphal tales of Reagan
rolling around on the Oval Office floor in laughter
as the plague swept through.
There had to be a cruel god's lightning bolts.

Indifference and its absence of signification
could not explain the body count.

And I learned of the once established truths
now known to be fiction.
Flight Attendant Gaetan Dugas:
The Patient Zero myth, a one man epidemic
sowing the seeds of disease from layover to layover.
There had to be a face
a Judas kiss framed by a 70s porn mustache
to vilify a viral protein structure.
There had to be a name,
the foreign French moaning unintelligibly
through contorted anglo mouths.
There had to be retribution
for freely realizing his desire,
a moment when his Air Canada plane
flew too close to the sun.

Despite every mapped genome
every milliliter of vaccine
every nuclear targeting of a cancer cell
every x-ray that shows us what's really inside,
superstition still fires silver bullets into the dark.
We are still afraid of getting it from a toilet seat,
still dying of metaphor.

The Blobfish

Psychrolutes marcidus
was never meant for terrestrial fame.
4,000 feet below in his own environment
without a gaseous bladder or bones,
he hovers listlessly above the ocean floor,
almost inert, drawing his mouth open only
to seduce prey. He isn't the javelin arched
dolphin or the serpentine eel, but he holds
the platonic form of a fish and
the crustaceans still know to beware.

Dredged up to the land from the depths,
his concentrated, yet gelatinous body
could not contain his expanding innards.
His once thin fishy frame bloated
beyond recognition and he assumed
the profile of the harangued everyman.

His mouth distended into a hapless frown,
bald pink skin sweating nervously
beneath the lamps in the laboratory,
beady little eyes dense with anxiety,
and that bulbous, flabby nose, probably
an organ squeezed through his brain,
lobotomized by the pressure shift.

I have met this fish many times before.
When I was ten, he lived in the aquarium
in my therapist's office. He'd bloop his frown
against the glass repeatedly as I tried to
draw my nightmares with waxy, clumpy
Roseart crayons they had instead of Crayolas.
Tropical fish swirled in their auroras
while the blobfish kept blooping,
blooping to read over my shoulder.
The scratch of the therapist's pen against
her ledger inscribed me like cuneiform
on a clay tablet and poked me down,
down into the couch, until
I lost myself between the cushions.

When the insurance money ran out,
I scooped the blobfish out of the tank,
and brought him home with me. We
flopped around in my inflatable pool
and when we gasped for breath, we
shared a few drags of my inhaler.

Six summers ago at Cornell,
he stared at me from my plate,
daring me to accidentally use
the salad fork to eat him.
Debates on post-structuralism
ricocheted across the ballroom
and compressed me down,
down into my chair, and my feet
dangled limp like the untied
shoelaces of a latchkey kid.

When the keynote on deontology
ended, I wrapped him up in a napkin
and brought him to my dorm room.
We split a Rolling Rock tall can and
hopped into the frying pan together.

The Rat King

Pulsing and scuttling in our walls,
a rat king forms as a nest population
exceeds the space for discrete individuals.
Babies are born destined for entanglement,
and the more they struggle to detach,
the tighter their tails tie together.

The heaving mass of knotted bodies
becomes one organism to survive.
They must never develop the nuance of mind
or process the impulse of subjectivity
that resists the momentum of mass.

The collective of whiskers directs
the wad of limbs forward through
the plumbing and electrical wires.
As the scurrying colony thumps
between slabs, I lie in bed,
assuming it's the rafters creaking
when humidity falls in the night.

Experienced carpenters know how
to knock on the walls and listen
for the swabbing mesh of tails
or the dull thud of a deceased rat king,
mummified and inflammable from years
of burrowing and breathing insulation.

Like layers of sedimentary rock,
the older bodies lie compressed
on the bottom. You can pinpoint
the time when the concretion of
corpses became too burdensome
for the living rats to pull towards food.
When they tried in vain to eat the dead,
and in their last days, when they tried to
eat each other:
feeling for the first time
in the conniption of teeth and claws,
the savagery of a self.

A Flamboyance

A flamingo father
produces pink milk
in his throat,
pours it perfectly
through his curved beak
into his chick's mouth.

His innately gray children
inherit his radiant pink.
But as they illuminate,
he fades slightly, drained
of the crustacean blush
that ignites his feathers.

As I read this
in *National Geographic*
I clutch my glass of rosé,
check the stone I've
been sitting on for years,
stretch my plumage,
and watch the red flush
of my nose light up
a mercifully barren room.

The Afterlife of Origami

I unfolded the wings
neck and beak
smoothed the creases
flattened the paper crane
into a single sheet, white
and unremarkable, no trace
of its avian anatomy or
the aerodynamics of flight
when it bent and glided
at the will of your fingers.

Its purity now a graffiti of crossed
out words, effacing everything
I wanted to say but drooled
and blotted the inked reasons.
It's a grocery list now
a catalog of banal needs
past the expiration date
to be wadded up
and forgotten in the cart.

A Standard Monkey Funeral on Sunset Boulevard

When I saw his lifeless hand
fall limp from the casket, I knew
I would follow him into the ground.
Only two pallbearers needed
for the procession, I wondered
with the velvet cushions, custom
gold and ivory inlay, why
it happened under the cover
of night. Who wasn't supposed
to hear the whispered eulogy?

At sunrise Los Angeles fastens
its veneers, chews the scenery
until what we call night remains.
Flashbulbs blind white, steal
a second of your life; the spots
before your eyes are stars seeing
their shadows. When they no longer
twinkled through your windows,
I held a flashlight to your face, crossed
two beams to the cracked ceiling:
a searchlight at a premiere
in your empty living room.

But at sunset, in the open backyard,
exposed to the fading limelight
of the firmament, a vigil may
arouse suspicion. Even a candle
on a tombstone rises like a lighthouse

searching for the wreck. To mourn
openly is to admit loss, to recognize
there are only so many impressions
of your face on the film, and when
the projector ends white, and the lights
turn on, the audience is free
to leave the theater.

Oxygen is Flowing to the Mask

At the exit of the airport security check
a drug sniffing K-9 found
one pill on the ground
ivory white ovular
a sequence of letters and numbers
etched in its face, decipherable
only to robots and pharmacists
trained to read
the alphabet of pain.

On the plane
I scan faces for the ache of an arthritic hip
the flush of a heart rate that will not ebb
the pulsing pupils and twitching eyebrows
the scratched wrists that itch to the marrow
the stonewashed eyes that sleep won't pardon.
It could be anyone's pill the dog had found.

As I sniffle under the recirculated air
taste only the sharp edge of a salt grain
on the pretzel stick, the scene from *Airplane!*
flashes before me:

> *What kind of a plane is it?*

*Oh, it's a big, pretty, white plane with red stripes,
curtains in the window, and wheels,
and it looks like a big Tylenol.*

We ride together in this capsule with wings
sliding in the sweat of withdrawals
slipping disks in choreographed turbulence.
Then we fall from the pocket, nose dive
to the floor, and bounce across the tile.
Dog breath fogging the windows.
We secure our own breathing apparatus first
though the bag may not inflate.

My Dog Begs For Something That Will Kill Her

She stares up at the counter
watching me hammer bricks
of baker's chocolate
into tiny daggers
as the double boiler hisses
to melt these cyanide chips
into velvety hemlock cocoa.

She flares her nostrils
licks her chops, props
her ears up to plead.
I've taught her the most
pathetic submission
will win her a cantaloupe rind
to gnaw, extra parmesan cheese
raining like manna on the tile,
the gristle end of the fatted calf,
the benevolence of by-products.

Sitting in the Food 4 Less cart
I cried when I could not have
the black licorice with the
dead cartoon rat. I dug
beneath the sink for the sweet
Pine Sol Kool-Aid, searched
shoeboxes for packets
of silica Sweet n' Low.

Because we ate from
the Tree of Knowledge
every poison berry drips
kissable on lush pouty lips.
How many times did someone
die eating the toxic fruit
around the cashew just to get
the nut inside? How many times
did they only want the fruit?

Despite the instinct of whines
and salivation, she trusts me
not to slither down from the
butcher block, offer a handful
of M&Ms and promise the
wisdom of mankind. She'd
only wake up, begging herself
for the pill wrapped in cheese.

Vegetative States

Medicinal Plants

Doris tells us, she's already mourning
the agave plant. The pups burgeoning
in the shade of its long broad leaves
show it will die within the year. Soon
a giant asparagus stalk will vault six feet
from the center, unfurl, and wither away.

Doris thought about the agave as her father
slept in his hospice bed. How beautiful
it would be if a flower sprouted
from his head and bloomed as he expired.

I worry about the fatherless pups budding
from the mattress. Will the orderlies know
to gather them as they strip the bed and scrub,
the smell of death from the metal instruments?

Will they resist the urge to water them too much?
The infrequent attention a desert plant needs
feels like neglect to those desperate to show care.

Doris points out the Royal Fern, explains
they haven't evolved since the Jurassic.
They've been run over by dinosaur feet
and tire treads, but their design survives
each age of lumbering masses.

Doris has to take this call. Her mother
cannot remember her docent schedule.

She must wash her pills down with buttermilk
or be found digging up the garden for
her father's depression era money can.

I worry about the uprooted bougainvillea waiting
every Tuesday afternoon to be replanted. Do they
retract their thorns out of kindness, knowing
that can is under an Iowa farm miles away?

Will Doris ever wonder why she never locks up
the pruning shears and shovels? She looks forward
to sharing the cool sting of aloe on scraped knuckles.

Cactus Needle

distanced but not protected
behind the camera lens
stinging tip broken
beneath the skin
in the tender pivot point
reverse the knuckle

carried to the city
the defensive desert
inflames handshakes
splinters the pencil grip
all things reached for
and desperate for caress

wait for white blood cells
to sense the infection
pus around the intruder
swell to the surface

under yellowing lamp
digging tweezer teeth
pulling a nerve threaded
through the eye of the spine

sterilized with gin
anesthetized with whiskey
cannot heal balled in a fist
only open in a sore offering

A Banyan Tree

I begin
a seed blown
lodged in the crack
of an upstanding tree
a rumor overheard
that infects the thinker.

I germinate unfelt
moored in scarred bark
long assumed healed
fed in a mossy crevice
unwashed unseen.

Born trunkless by nature
my wooden fingers emerge
and cling to his limbs
a hairy knuckled grasp
against the wind.

As I mature my vines
caress down his trunk
and enmesh him coiling
my gnarled tentacles
until he disappears.

I become the forest they see
the bandages wrapped
around breathing mummies
mistaken for the pharaoh's skin.

They say I hide my fraudulence
in plain view, a parasite that
swallows the host whole
then takes his place. But this
has always been a land of invaders.

My limbs are boas sliming
through the Everglades
my roots planted firmly like
a conquistador's flag pole.

I swarm the land like a red tide
rhizome like turnpikes
and multiply like condos
colonizing the shore.

Drought in Los Angeles

Pulling into the driveway, he sees
the dirt patches expanded in the lawn,
checks his hairline in the rear view mirror,
and glances at the coiled garden hose,
defanged and prohibited from use. He feels
the blades of grass ebbing from his scalp
as the sun refuses to hide behind the sycamores.

He surveys the abandoned family garden.
The marigolds birthed with a shrug
could not support their heads
and died bent over among the wilted petunias
mourned by the endangered panda expression
on the shriveled pansies.

Beneath the air conditioner,
an intermittent drip where one dandelion
clings to the soil with serrated leaves.
He picks the weed and blows the spores
wishing the comb over would take root
a wispy coat of baby chick down to frost
where the veined faultline cracks through.

American Gothic

Nan Wood was embarrassed
her brother paired her
with a man twice her age

and told anyone who would listen
the painting was of father and daughter

he guards his aging little girl
with a politefully stern
midwestern stare

she looks grimly sideways
into the distant modernism
barred by the pitchfork

her distended neck
and oval head
an American Modigliani
with all the realism
of the rutted earth
plowed across her face

better a spinster
gazing past the corn
than the wife
unpictured in the kitchen

Haying

after Grant Wood's painting

At full day the farmer surveys his work.
The walls of threshed hay form a labyrinth
etching a map of his labor into the land.

The trail is his own, but he cannot remember
the route. He tries to retrace his raked steps
but at every turn a dead end bricked in hay.

He looks to the barn in the distance, his point
of origin at dawn, wonders how he strayed
so far away into the peripheral landscape.

Why his every morning straight and narrow
serpentines into the hissing evening, leaving
him winding home, afraid to kick over the stacks.

How at sundown the textured horizon weaves
itself with loose straw before his bleary eyes
and the bladed windmill reaps swaths of dusk.

Spilt Milk

after Grant Wood's painting

All the good ideas I ever had came to me while I was milking a cow.
  - Grant Wood.

The cow is ashamed
her limp neck droops
to the ground, unwilling
to support her head
and the feral impulse
it shot down her spine.

Before she could reason
she kicked the can
and the boy drips
in milk and shock.

She has learned from the dog.
Her upturned eyes implore
the farmer for forgiveness.
She knows she has broken
the unwritten contract
of domestication.

10,000 years of animal husbandry
has bred her horns into nubs.
Her udder swells daily with more milk
than her calves could possibly drink.

The fence around the barn
no longer keeps her in,
but keeps the wilderness out.

She knows in exchange
for the providence of alfalfa
and the safety of the farmer's rifle
she becomes a product.

But breeding can never
extinguish the flickering
of Mrs. O'Leary's lamp
igniting her instinct.

A Boy and His Piñata

Once we banned the barbaric practice of clubbing
baby piñatas, they aged into full adults for the first time.
Surplus populations brayed and spat in party store
windows waiting for adoption as their rainbow paper
coats faded in the sun. Others were bid upon
at livestock auctions, their waded newspaper muscles
graded prime before selling the breeding rights.

Daddy told me not to get attached.
There are pets, and there are worker animals.
Birthday clowns and business clowns.
But Jenny ruffled like a ball gown as she led
the plow team and I collected handfuls of Skittles
left in small piles dotting the field.

The stable hay was too coarse
for her construction paper skin, so I hoisted her
from the rafters. Daddy knew I sneaked
off at night to brush her and feed her Starbursts
from my palm. She never bit or spit, just
kicked in the air like an origami pegasus
flying through a fifth grader's diorama.

When harvest season came, Jenny grew sluggish
could barely stand on her legs or walk out the barn.
Soon, her side ran raw with sores, pink syrupy pus
leaking. Might have been strawberry or cherry.
You can never tell based on color alone.

The vet massaged his finger through her stapled,
cardboard seam and felt the massive lump
of melted chocolate congealed around
the plastic kazoos and little green army men inside:
the ambergris of my childhood
too large to pass through her intestines.

He offered the gas, but Daddy waved him away
motioned at me to enter:

> *You chose to bond with her.*
> *She's your responsibility*

He handed me a baseball bat, spun me three times,
and though he told me not to, I peaked
from beneath the blindfold, met Jenny's gaze
eye to googly eye. When I swung she knew
not to rise on the rope, but remain still, close her eyes,
and dream of flying through fields of birthday cake.

Hollywood Camouflage

At the Burbank Lockheed factory
my great-grandfather built P-38s hidden
beneath a fake farm. The Total War era
meant battlefields without bounds
and combattants on assembly lines.

Hollywood set designers draped netting
over the buildings, painted runways and
parking lots green, rigged trees with wire
and feathers, brush strokes of fake decay
a pastoral matte board to fool any pilots
searching above for the war engine.

The plant managers directed their labor
choreographed small shifts in and out
hid smoke breaks in an empty silo.
Workers pinned their family's laundry
on the clothesline between hours of welding.

Great-Grandfather was a Dust Bowl Okie
and all the young women asked him for tips.
How would a farm girl swing her hips as she
walked? Would her drawl drip slowly from
her lips? Is this frilly apron believable?

He tried to tell them, he was a repairman
from Guymon, shop belly up in the Depression.
He could teach them soldering and repair, but
they knew how to keep a pneumatic from

recoiling, confident in their Rosie the Riveter
muscles pumping with the pistons on the line.

He came to realize, the acting was their hope.
Warner Brothers and Universal Studios were
just down the road, but worlds away during war
when you're rationing sugar and nylons.
He showed them a photo of his daughters,
their hair in two long braids like Judy Garland,
so they too could skip from sepia into technicolor.

Victory Garden

Used aluminum foil
unwaded, pressed smooth
with a rolling pin, filed
in the drawer by length.

Ziploc bags inverted
wiped of remains
clothespinned to dry.

She tells me
during the war
industrial white margarine bars
came with yellow dye capsules
to crush and imitate
butter's oily sunshine.

You whipped til your elbow throbbed
if you wanted a thin spread of
luxury, a little grease to ease
the burnt toast down your throat.

You whipped til it felt like churning,
til visions of the battlefield whirled
around in the kitchen and
appliances rattled like machine guns.

We didn't know the Butter Lobby
got yellow dyed margarine banned
by the government well before the war.
We thought we were doing our part.

She grabs the half-full Costco
sized margarine tub on the table.
Her pupils pulse
like they're counting
dart like they're adding.

When I'm gone, this should be
about big enough to hold my ashes.
Mix me with the compost and the
leftover casseroles at the wake.
Spread me evenly among the roses.

Produce in a Pandemic

It's 1990,
the cold metal bars
in the shopping cart child's seat
are a quiet relief from
the San Fernando Valley sun.
In the market, I see pyramids
of gleaming ruby apples, uniformly waxed.
Grandma knocks on watermelons
puts her ear to the rind, listening
for something an octave lower than
the Muzak anesthetizing the store, lower
than the bored drone of fluorescent lights.
Something I could not hear.

It's 2020,
Grandma is quarantined
in the same house she bought in 1959.
The fields outside her windows
that reminded her of native Oklahoma
paved over for an airport. The wealthy
still buzz over in luxury jets, their exhaust
coloring her swimming pool slightly grey.

She texts me her grocery list, the first time
she's ever asked me for anything, ever.
> Two bags of greens
> > (The parakeets prefer kale)
> A nice baking potato
> Half n' Half for coffee

        Three ripe avocados
        Mylanta, if they still make that
        And a nice melon for breakfast
This is more than just the list:
this is the moment I was raised for,
everything I should have been studying
watching from the cart seat, her eyes
carefully studying the nutrition labels
comparing the ounce per dollar prices,
instead of being mesmerized by the Toucan Sam
following my nose to childhood diabetes
crying until I was catatonic for Cocoa Puffs.
I learned that generic Malt-O-Meal
Marshmallow Mateys and Good Enuff Puffs
were a delayed "I love you." A sensibly priced
breakfast later meant money for soccer cleats,
a summer popsicle from the ice cream man.

I am ready,
my old underwear mask tied
across my face like a ninja, I stealthily
cut through the 99 Cent Store,
dodging coughers left, produce gropers right.
This is what I spent 30 years training for:
the Home Ec final taken during a fire evacuation.

They don't have Mylanta, but I know she'll love
America's Pride brand liquid antacid because it's 99 cents
and the flimsy bottle means more chalk for your buck.
The Half n' Half available is a miracle,
no cans of condensed milk as a substitute,
no memories of ration cards, no WWII flashbacks

to a church key, saucer pan on the stove,
infant sister crying for something better.
Three avocados, hard like green dinosaur eggs:
You'll have your guacamole in 5-7 days, Grandma.
No kale, but among these three different
mixes of salad, kale is the 3rd or 4th listed
ingredient. The parakeets can kick the iceberg
and romaine to the newspaper lined floor.
A baking potato is not chosen for ripeness,
but for a skin that will tan, crackle in the oven,
the innards blistering through, puffy golden,
I grab five, wipe the soiled prints off my hands.

Then the final boss
The melon:
I grab a cantaloupe: bald and spotted
like Grandpa's head, and I knock
dull thuds, signifying nothing.
I pick another, knock on Grandpa's head
hoping to hear his voice:

>how to fasten a bolo tie
>
>how to replace a fuse
>
>how to smooth the grout between tiles

something that tells me what's inside.

I remember him in the VA hospital
foggy eyes glazed off into the distance
how I knocked, knock, knock,
knocking on his brain with my questions
hoping to hear something resonate from inside.
He saw the TV from the distance:

>*The greens aren't guarding the reds*

The blurred abstraction of Michigan St. v. Ohio St.
and it was true, the Buckeyes were dominating the paint
and we discussed, the triangle offense, John Wooden
and the proper form for a free throw before he slept
and I never saw him wake up.

I palm the cantaloupe like a basketball
imagine shooting it into the cart, with perfect form
from just outside the dairy case, hoping Grandma
will hear the swish when she opens the bag.

I leave her groceries on the porch,
can only see her through the screen door.
I remember before we got air conditioning,
how the cool breeze through the screen
on a summer night in the valley
brought sweet deliverance as we watched
the weather forecast through the waves of static.
Now I see her on the screen, just as obscured
and distanced, projected in low definition
but her warm glow forged in the dust bowl
still reflects on my glasses.

Zoonomia

Your Mother Doesn't Want You Wasting Color Film on Zebras

Feel free to spend your film on boulders
mistaken for galapagos tortoises,
the fleshy eclipse of a thumb
obscuring a monkey, the anonymous
neck of a giraffe decapitated
by the viewfinder, or the pigeons
pecking your trail of dropped popcorn
even though we can see them
at the corner park for free.

Color film is for the pink haze
of a flamingo across the lagoon
in a distant flamboyance,
the captured yawn of a tiger
remembered as a roar.

But most of all, do not waste
your color film on zebras. They live
in an impossible world of black and white
contrast, defined binaries and geometries.
A baby zebra imprints on her mother's
stripes, memorizes the pattern, follows
its map for life across the dusty savanna.
Zookeepers can copy the stripes, paint
them on t-shirts, and lead the baby zebra
anywhere by the gravity of instinct.

Do not trace the familiarity of my veins
when you should be scribbling off paper.
Zebras are born with a predestined
ending always after the xylophone
or x-ray. They always know their place
in the taxonomy of all living beings,
but it comes at the price of accepting
they're the untouched page in the coloring book.

The Inquisitor's Parrots

When Columbus returned to Spain,
he gifted two parrots to Queen Isabella.
History cannot tell us how long it took
until the birds had forgotten the language
of the Taíno they mimicked on the island
and if the Spaniards ever registered those
sounds as distinct words or assumed
they were meaningless squawks.

We do not know if the sailors, tired of hearing
the parrots screech for home, stowed them deep
in the brig, where they slept a four month night
or if they bonded with their captors, perched on
their shoulders, and learned the Spanish tongue.

The are no records of their lives in Spain
or what they witnessed in the royal councils.
We do not know if they were bribed with olives
to teach them to shriek *auto da fe, auto da fe,*
as the condemned was mortified before the crowd
or if the parrots themselves ended their lives
on the braziers, having revealed too much.

Great Hall of the Bulls

In the caves of Lascaux, we come to hear
the stampede of aurochs reverberating
through the ancient hall: the trace of their outlines
in earthen pigments, the first finger of man
flattening the wilderness into points and lines.
The invented myth of a lost origin
when men were men
and beasts were beasts
and men were beasts,
but beasts weren't men.

In 1627, we recorded the last auroch
to stomp and rut across central Europe.
He roamed through teutonic mythology
etched into wood blocks above the altschrift
emblazoned on medieval coats of arms.
Caesar said they were as big as elephants;
they ate the grass grown between his ruins.

In the 30s, German brothers Heinz and Lutz Heck
tried to revive the auroch from the error of extinction.
They believed the science of breeding back
could resurrect the auroch from the genes
of domestic cattle. Artificially select
the most aggressive specimen and inject
the snarl of the wild back into the bull.

Hermann Goring envisioned stocking
his hunting preserve with a herd
of primeval beasts: A theme park where
the Nazi elite could live their fantasies
of a pristine prussian past, prancing
through the forest with Erl Kings
and magical flutes thanks to the inevitable
progress of eugenics, reveling in the peaty
uncontaminated dung of the mulish bull
whose violent instinct became their ideology:
the purer the brute, the more noble their stomp.

Amidst the rubble and ashes of the reich
a handful of Heck cattle survived WWII,
too wild for the ranch, too tame for the forest.
A few farmers still breed them as a novelty,
a replica of the relic now old enough for its
own pedestal. A witness who hears in his DNA,
not the bellow of his ancestor's call
shaking branches in the Black Forest
but the bombs above the Tiergarten
and the screams behind the gate.

The Vulture and the Little Girl

after Kevin Carter's photograph

Framed in the foreground
a body too atrophied to stand
bent forward as if praying.

The vulture gazed at the child
not in hunger, but as if aware
of his symbolic perch.

The photographer assured us
he shooed away the bird
moments after snapping the image.

But he never learned the girl
was actually a boy
or that he would survive
the trek to the famine relief station
and live into his teens.

The photographer left Sudan,
but the vulture followed him
home to Johannesburg.

He hovered in the darkroom
as the memories of war
and violence and death
developed beneath the red light.

And when all he could see of the world
were the atrocities reflected on the lens
the photographer took one last shot
as the vulture stood vigil.

The Law of the Tongue

In the Eden Killer Whale Museum
Old Tom's skeleton hangs
spine propped by poles
rods fusing the bones.

Stripped of his skin, blubber,
and muscles, the sleek curves
and color patterns that make Orcas
theme park stars, his predator core
is revealed. That fin waving hello
above the water, long ago rotted away.
The skull has a gator's sharp snout
bearing an incomplete snarl of teeth.
He is jagged and hard in death.

Old Tom earned his name working
with the whalers in Twofold Bay.
He tail-slapped the mouth
of the Kiah River, alerting the men
when a pod of baleen whales
was ready for slaughter.
He herded them to the surface
as the whalers readied their harpoons.
Sometimes he'd pull the ropes
if they were slow in pursuit.

Old Tom was paid in kind
by The Law of the Tongue:
the unspoken arrangement
leaving him first dibs
on the fresh kill's lips and tongue.

He died after losing teeth
in a tug of war with a fisherman
who did not obey the law.
The orcas left the bay
after the betrayal,
and Tom's starved corpse
washed ashore years later.

If you can look Tom face to face
you will see through the hole
in his grin, down his ribcage,
and past his vertebrae to where the tail
has decomposed and vanished.
Waving out the other end,
tourists see you framed in the hole.

The Desert Snail at Once Awoke and Found Himself Famous

This particular mollusk, at the time of his arrival in London, was really alive and vigorous. But as the authorities of the British Museum, to whose tender care he was consigned, were ignorant of this important fact, he was gummed, mouth downward, onto a piece of cardboard, and duly labelled and dated with scientific accuracy, 'Helix desertorum, March 25, 1846.

- Grant Allen, *Seven Year Sleepers* (1889)

Shipped thousands of miles from Egypt,
the desert snail spent four years
trapped in his own shell
beneath a glass in the British Museum
unaware of half interested glances,
making their way through the room toward
more curious antiquities and marvels.
A metal suit of armor gleaming down the hall,
its inhabitant, centuries ago scooped from
the recesses of its shell, the life once inside
still as anonymous as the snail sealed asleep
in its own chambers.

Documented, classified, and arranged
with teleological precision
among the other dead specimen,
the snail was placed in exact distance
in the timeline from a plump stuffed dodo,
face reshaped after death with a dumb expression,
welcoming the Portuguese explorers to her island.
But the snail was not supposed to be a cautionary tale,
just a necessary acquisition in the noble pursuit
of the knowledge of all things.

Just as the curators took for granted
the vacant content of the shell,
we assume the snail had no interior life.
Its indifferent slime tracks across the
dog-headed gods in the hieroglyphics
chipped off the tomb and shipped to Britain
to decipher our evolution in the delta.
How it retreated inward and impersonated a rock
when the plagues of locusts swarmed
and the sky rained blood and hungry toads.
How it tucked itself away amidst the blasts
when Napoleon shot the nose off the Sphinx.

Years after the cardboard label began to discolor,
the curators realized their error and revived
the desert snail in a warm bath. When Grant Allen
documented this history, he described:

> *the grateful snail,*
> *waking up at the touch of the familiar moisture,*
> *put his head cautiously out of his shell, walked*
> *up to the top of the basin, and began to take a*
> *cursory survey of British institutions with his four*
> *eye-bearing tentacles.*

And he editorialized:
> *who shall say hereafter that science is unfeeling!*

Maybe serious, maybe ironic; I will never be sure.
I am deaf to the flourishes of his 19th century tone
and Mr. Allen was long ago buried in England,
sealed up and stored away in his casket.

P.T. Barnum Presents the Egress

A French Poodle in a tutu
backflips through a flaming hoop.

A monkey with glasses and a cigar
waves and imitates the governor.

A tiger balanced on stacked chairs
remembers who delivers his meat.

A bear in a fez loses control of his
tricycle and runs over a clown.

A lion locks his jaw as the tamer
plunges his head into the void.

But none of these spectacles compare
to the exotic lure of the egress.

The signs point: This Way To The Egress!
and the mystery beast behind the door.

We hurry through to see the horns, talons,
fangs, fire breathing, primal roar of the egress.

Push and shove our way through, elbows
thrown at the ribs, steel toe to the achilles.

Only to find ourselves, out the exit, door
slammed behind, piled atop each other.

In the alley, the mass of the crowd waiting
for something to happen. Quit hoggin'

the egress! You're blocking my view of the egress!
I paid good money to see this egress, jackass!

We'll throw fists, point fingers, curse, and accuse
searching for the beast in the belly of the egress.

The Art of Preparing, Mounting, and Stuffing the Skins

In the Sportsman's Lodge
every hunting trophy is staged
in a moment of ferocity. The drama
of the wild costumed through the parlor.
The buck's head sloped downward
eyes forward, ready to charge
from the wooden plaque
above the men's room.
The bear towering on two legs
claws raised as if challenging you
in arm to arm combat.
The back fur raised on the fox
The polished snarl of the boar
The swordfish arched shouting *en garde*

You never see them laid to rest
eyes sewn shut in the merciful sleep
of a casket bed. Even Lenin stuffed
in his glass mausoleum isn't posed
boldly staring into the brave red future
or handing wheat stocks to peasants,
but lying, arms folded in a worker's slumber.

When the hunter dies we burn evidence
he was ever made of bone, hair, and meat.
On the mantle, it is never certain, which
is the urn and which is the bowling trophy.

But looming above in the sun faded
Sears Portrait Studio photo, his stance
of patriarchal benevolence is enshrined
stuffed in a sweater vest, his glasses,
slightly drooped down his nose
so you can't see the reflection
of the photographer who posed him.

A Taxidermist and a Mortician Walk into a Bar

The taxidermist gestures to the dusty old buck's head
over the pool table and calls it a hack job. His eyes
are pointed too close together like he's going to sneeze
and shoot the cobwebs from his nose.

The mortician motions to a couple sipping martinis
across the bar: both masked in radioactive complexions
of Dorito dust spray tans. Points out the thin pallid line
between the temples and hairlines.

When they bring in a buck, they want me to recreate
some majestic pose of nobility and strength they've seen
drawn on a snuff can. Suture the wounds in the back
tightly, so you can't tell he was shot from behind
tranquilly lapping from a stream.

When they bring in a man, shotgun blast up through the jaw
it's not the toupee over the exit wound that concerns them,
but if I can sew back his lonely hangdog jowls into a smile
brush enough warming rouge across his sleepless eye bags
to make it look like a young heart attack.

The taxidermist picks up the check, so he can place the
two quarters in change over his eyes: *look at me, I'm*
gonna ride the ferry to Hades. The mortician puts his
thumbs on his temples, fingers mimicking moose antlers.
The taxidermist points his finger gun and shoots the mortician
in the patch of white between his eyes.

Bees that Feed on Human Tears

They're not the architects
  plotting the angles of the hive
They're not the drones
  hammering the honeycomb
  into a commune of hexagons
They're not the pollinators
  tickling stamens field to field
They're not the confectioners
  sugaring the walls with saliva
They're not the queen
  orchestrating the swarm

They're not the buzz
  nor the bumble

They are the stifle
  and the sniffle

They are the stingers
  mistaken for a loose eyelash
They are the mute antennae
  always dialed between the channels
They are the dam beneath the eyelid
  the swelling of what cannot be purged
They are the fog on the lens
  pixelating smiling wrinkles on a face
They are the tattooer's needle
  the pang of the present made permanent

Coal Mine Canaries

By 1986, the British mining companies
released the last of the coal mine canaries.
Like many of its fellow proletarians,
automation stole the canary's livelihood.
The mines installed digital noses to detect
the odorless spectre of carbon monoxide.

The canary union protested:
we do more than faint and warn
of impending death.
We sang for the miners, chirping
renditions of pop hits miles deep
where radio waves could not penetrate.
We were a flickering of the world above:
a beam of feathers shining through the crags.

But there was no use
fighting Margaret Thatcher in the 80s,
so the canaries read the classifieds
lining the bottom of their cages.
Some fluttered about Chernobyl
until the radiation made them molt,
and fall naked into the elephant's foot.
They flew to the uranium mines,
but as they glowed ominously neon,
the unshielded miners shrugged
and kept digging.

Other canaries braved the flight
across the Atlantic to Washington DC
as the AIDS quilt was stitched
across the National Mall,
and began plummeting from the sky.
They flew to the White House
and startled Nancy Reagan,
crashing into her bedroom window.
She watched them in her nightgown,
as they one by one hit the glass
and scattered across the lawn.
When the janitor swept them into a heap,
she cracked a reassured smile
as he whistled slightly out of tune.

Earthquake Weather

The cicadas are the warning alarm
for an earthquake that never strikes.
Primate hair bristles through me
vigilant in the emergency hissing.
Throbbing beneath the undergrowth
the ground writhes like the wormed
belly of a stray dog. Bones clatter
and kick their way to the surface,
knitting through the brush
> a hornet in the bladder
> a hemorrhaging of memory
> an odorless rupture in the pipe.

The inflamed red behind the eyelid
when the skinned knee glare of the
irate sun penetrates the drawn shade.

The faultline veined
across the cracked sidewalk
helicopters slice the sky, and peer
into the anthill, filming what we've long
forgotten we buried, the knotted
dirt clods in my back, my shovel tip
knocking on the casket door.

Shooting the Janitor

The Turkey Vulture does not understand
how when we look to the sky for omens
we cannot see the life behind the symbol,
the blocked artery beneath the heartbreak.
He does not know we hear his call as a dirge
that his patience is confused for prophesy
that he looms over the festering of guilt.

Gliding above, unaware he is a harbinger
people below chart the geometry of his loops
trace his flight pattern with their fingers
hoping to spell out a name, something he knows
about the ground he circles, and the longer you
watch, the more you perceive he circles you.

But the Turkey Vulture is not the Grim Reaper's
falcon, running errands for the doomed. His prey
is carrion, those animals who long ago

>   keeled over belly full of pesticide,
>   collided off the front bumper,
>   lapped antifreeze trickling down the arroyo,
>   managed to limp further after the buckshot

and saw the face beneath the hood was man
and his scythe was an aerosol can.

He looks for putrefaction, meat spoiled
to the point of danger. He can eat salmonella
without illness, clean the streets of botulism
and anthrax with only a beak and stomach.

No, the Turkey Vulture isn't coming for us.
He is the coroner and the janitor swooping in
long after we've fled the scene. He swallows
our casualties, and digests the evidence.

The Falling Iguanas

The year I lived on the beaches of Fort Lauderdale,
in January, the city council issued a warning:
beware of frozen iguanas falling from the trees.

At 50 degrees Fahrenheit, an iguana's metabolism
slows to the point of paralysis. Its limbs stiffen,
and a swift gust of wind can sweep it off a branch.

Do not cradle it in your arms like a forsaken infant,
though you may see your unfulfilled ambitions
reflected in its cold scales and glassed over eyes.

Do not bring it in your home and draw it a warm bath.
Do not crochet it a tiny woolen sweater. Do not mix it
a margarita and think it will empathize with your regrets.

The iguana can reanimate and attack you at any moment.
Even though they are not Florida natives, their instincts
have learned the bite or be bitten order of the land.

By law, the Florida conservationists cannot use evolution
to explain why iguanas cannot survive the cold, but they
can tell us God housed them in Latin America for a reason.

Iguanas are an invasive species, smuggled from their land
to be pets, gawked at in a glass box, inert and slimy under
a heat lamp like a tray of buffalo wings at a strip club buffet.

When they escaped, some ventured to the swamp lands
forming truces with the gators. Others ran to the golf resorts
amusing foreign businessmen scuttling after rolling grapes.

Though the iguanas adapted to the culture, they cannot
keep up with the changing climate. But the conservationists
must say this is God's way of fixing our invasive species problem.

As the iguana carcasses pile on your lawn, remember, ice ages
happen every 10,000 years, and that giant sloths who ate
avocados and passed the pit whole, used to slowly roam Florida.

The Battle of the Zoo

Knautschke the hippo was born in Berlin
amidst the blitzkriegs and firebombings
of late World War Two. The Nazis
turned the zoo into a fort, built a flak tower
on the perimeter: one of the last bastions
of retreat against the advancing allies.

When artillery ignited his animal house
zookeepers rushed to save Knautschke,
evacuated him into the bunker where he saw
Nazi soldiers bleeding out, their families
shaking and cowering in the shell shock.

After the bombing, the bars of the cages
were gnarled and twisted. 30% of the animals
heaped dead; the others hid in the rubble or escaped
wandering the topography of the toppled city.
Zookeepers grabbed rifles, hunted the predators,
fearing they would attack the reich from within.
But hippos are herbivores so Knautschke
was spared: a benign giant lumbering
through the fall of the fatherland.

Through the maelstrom Knautschke survived:
> When the Allies won and the Nazis
> abandoned him
> When the Russian soldiers ran out of food
> and slaughtered most of the remaining
> animals.

>   When the conspirators could not justify
>   just following orders and hung at Nuremberg.

After the war and reconstruction, the old iron bars
and concrete floors were demolished for a new
design replicating the wild's natural environment.
The spectacle of marveling at primitive oddities
replaced with the veneer of conservation.
Parents led their children, born of ashes and ruins,
heirs to the unspoken, through the new zoo,
watched Knautschke happy in his new home,
chomping cabbages, swimming daintily in a grace
only possible in water. The innocent buoyancy
of such great mass made it seem to those
remembering the ponderous goose steps they strode
and the rumbling tanks they cheered
like it was possible all such crushing weights
could lift on their own and float away.

Koko the Gorilla Signs in the Afterlife

and she asks God
why she was given
knuckles that drag the ground
and a mind that questions the sky.

Sentience,
consciousness of her own existence.
The faculty of object permanence
in a world where all objects must pass.
A kitten to love
to raise
to guard
to find lifeless beneath the tire swing.
To feel the stab of loss
without the rituals of grief.

Eyes that can see all the shades of grey
in the depression rainbow.
The overcast horizon of melancholia
framed by the chain links of a fence.
But only the sign language of
    Koko wants banana
To express it all.

Koko wants banana
(What happened to my mother when we were separated?)

Koko wants banana
(Where does the Earth go when we dream?)

Koko wants banana
(Do gorillas in the wild scream about syringes in their sleep?)

Koko wants banana
(Why did Robin Williams kill himself
even though he was so happy when I met him?)

Koko wants banana
(When King Kong fell from the Empire State Building,
did visions of frolicking through the grasses of Skull Island
rush through his brain before it splattered across 5th Ave?)

Koko wants banana
(Why do we use words if we can't possess the ideas they describe?)

She learns
the only sign language
God knows
is a shrug.

Chase Dimock lives among mountain lions and coyotes in an undisclosed location between Laurel Canyon and the Hollywood Hills of Los Angeles. He serves as the Managing Editor of *As It Ought To Be Magazine* and makes his living teaching literature and writing at College of the Canyons. His poetry has been published in *Waccamaw, Hot Metal Bridge, Faultline, Roanoke Review, New Mexico Review,* and *Flyway* among others. He holds a PhD in Comparative Literature from the University of Illinois and his scholarship and reviews in World Literature and LGBT Studies have appeared in *College Literature, Western American Literature, Modern American Poetry, The Lambda Literary Review,* and several academic anthologies. For more, visit chasedimock.com

This project was made possible, in part, by generous support from the Osage Arts Community.

Osage Arts Community provides temporary time, space and support for the creation of new artistic works in a retreat format, serving creative people of all kinds — visual artists, composers, poets, fiction and nonfiction writers. Located on a 152-acre farm in an isolated rural mountainside setting in Central Missouri and bordered by ¾ of a mile of the Gasconade River, OAC provides residencies to those working alone, as well as welcoming collaborative teams, offering living space and workspace in a country environment to emerging and mid-career artists. For more information, visit us at www.osageac.org

www.ingramcontent.com/pod-product-compliance
Lightning Source LLC
Chambersburg PA
CBHW020617130526
44592CB00054B/770